This book belongs to:

To my mom and my dad,
to endless patience.

– A.N.

Ancient Wonders © Flying Eye Books 2019.

First edition published in 2019 by Flying Eye Books,
an imprint of Nobrow Ltd. 27 Westgate Street, London E8 3RL.

Illustrations © Avalon Nuovo 2019.
Avalon Nuovo has asserted her right under the Copyright, Designs
and Patents Act, 1988, to be identified as the Illustrator of this Work.

Iris Volant is the pen name of the Flying Eye Books in-house writers.
Text written by Avalon Nuovo.

Every attempt has been made to ensure any statements written as fact have
been checked to the best of our abilities. However, we are still human, thankfully,
and occasionally little mistakes may crop up. Should you spot any errors, please
email info@nobrow.net.

10 9 8 7 6 5 4 3 2 1

Published in the US by Nobrow (US) Inc.
Printed in Poland on FSC® certified paper.

MIX
Paper from
responsible sources
FSC www.fsc.org FSC® C002795

ISBN: 978-1-912497-91-1
www.flyingeyebooks.com

Iris Volant & Avalon Nuovo

ANCIENT WONDERS

FLYING EYE BOOKS

London | New York

CONTENTS

No one knows quite who decided the Seven Wonders of the Ancient World but centuries of historians, poets, and philosophers wrote thrilling accounts of their wonder, leaving us to ponder their great mysteries.

Today, we know these seven ancient wonders as the Great Pyramid of Giza, the Hanging Gardens of Babylon, the Temple of Artemis at Ephesus, the Statue of Zeus at Olympia, the Mausoleum at Halicarnassus, the Colossus of Rhodes, and the Lighthouse of Alexandria. They have captured the imaginations of scholars and dreamers for generations, showing the great power and ingenuity of the ancient civilizations that built them . . . but these are only a few of the many stunning artworks of civilizations past!

Go on a journey across the world and through time, as we explore these and many more impressive monuments, the ingenious technology that made them possible, and the devoted people who worked tirelessly to bring them to life. These are . . . ancient wonders.

THE GREAT PYRAMID OF GIZA

Circa 2575–2465 BCE

Just west of the Egyptian city of Giza, a great stone guardian towers above the horizon—the Great Pyramid. Built four and a half thousand years ago, this massive monument is the oldest of all seven ancient wonders, and the only one that still exists today.

The Great Pyramid was built as a tomb for the pharaoh Khufu. A pharaoh was considered to be someone between god and man, and it was very important that his spirit had a successful journey to the afterlife. The pharaoh's pyramid would have been built to protect his body and show the grandeur of his reign, but corridors were also constructed to help guide him to the afterlife.

At nearly 500 feet tall and 750 feet wide on each side, the Pyramid of Khufu (as it is also known) took enormous groups of Egyptian workers somewhere between 10 and 20 years to complete, and remained the tallest building in the world for more than 3,000 years after it was built. Its four equal sides are exactly aligned with the directions of the compass, and its four corners are nearly perfect right angles. This still baffles builders and historians today, because ancient Egyptians did all of this without modern technology like iron tools, pulleys, or even wheels!

INSPIRATION: ANCIENT EGYPTIAN DEITIES

At the time of Khufu's reign, the ancient Egyptians had strong beliefs about death and the afterlife. These were intertwined with their religion, which included a pantheon of gods and goddesses.

According to their beliefs, when a person died, his or her body had to be properly preserved in order for their spirit-self to proceed safely to the afterlife. This would happen in a process known as "mummification." He or she would then have to pass through a series of fearsome tests as they journeyed through the underworld before finally appearing in front of the god Osiris.

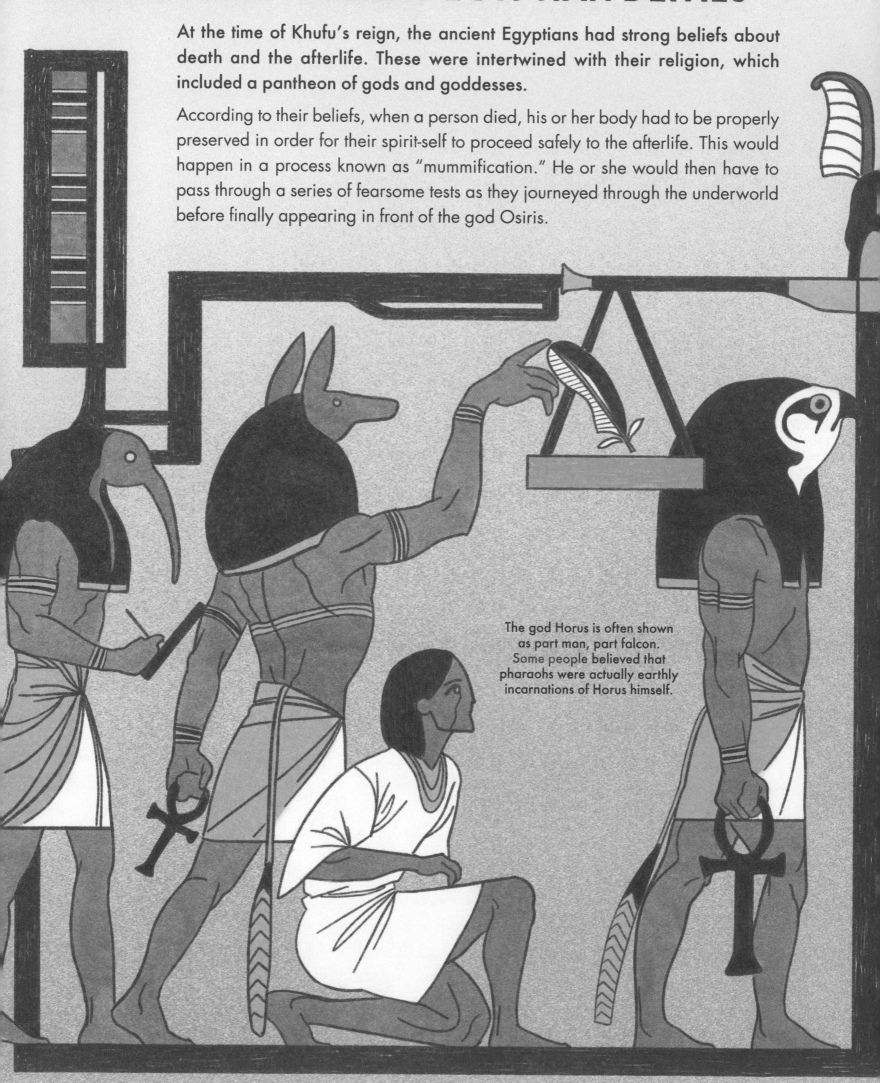

The god Horus is often shown as part man, part falcon. Some people believed that pharaohs were actually earthly incarnations of Horus himself.

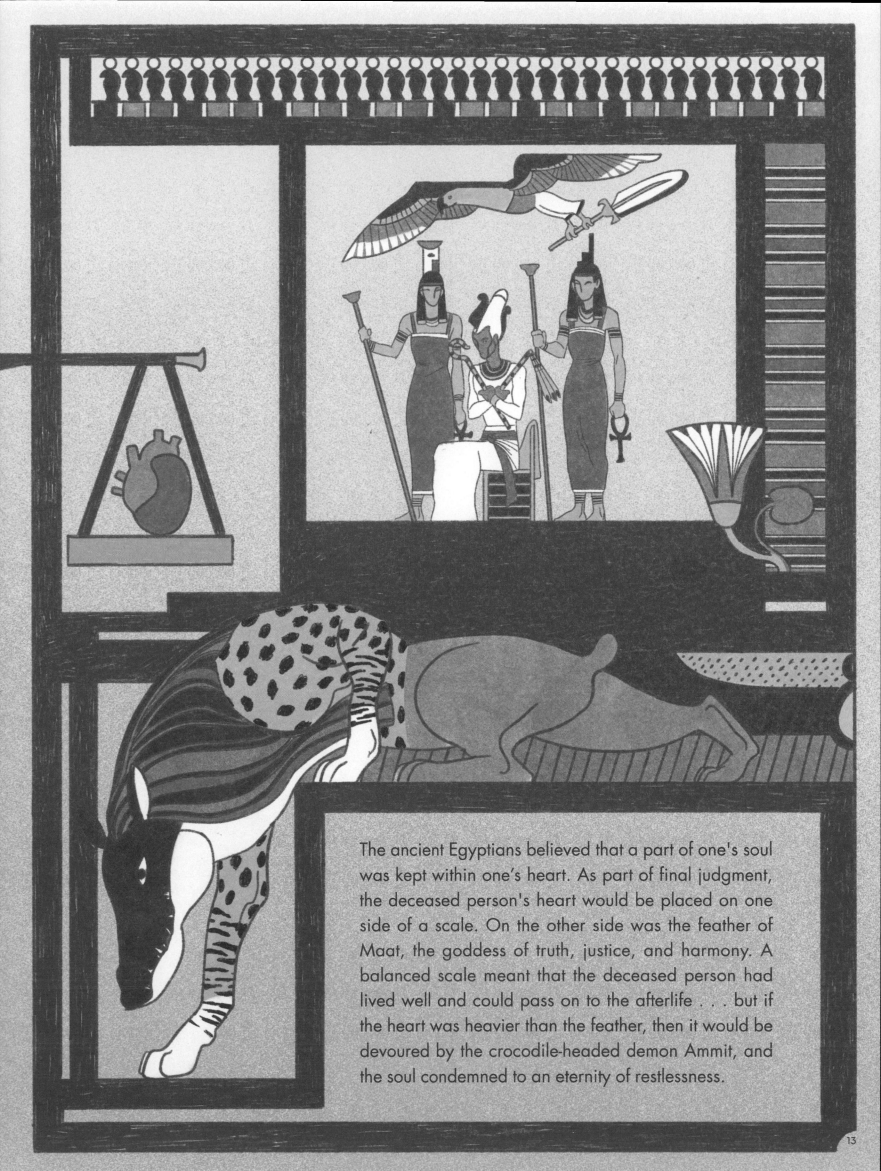

The ancient Egyptians believed that a part of one's soul was kept within one's heart. As part of final judgment, the deceased person's heart would be placed on one side of a scale. On the other side was the feather of Maat, the goddess of truth, justice, and harmony. A balanced scale meant that the deceased person had lived well and could pass on to the afterlife . . . but if the heart was heavier than the feather, then it would be devoured by the crocodile-headed demon Ammit, and the soul condemned to an eternity of restlessness.

INSIDE THE GREAT PYRAMID

We are able to continue exploring the Great Pyramid as it still stands today. Even so, its curious system of tunnels and chambers remain a mystery. Some historians believe that they exist simply because the pharaoh Khufu kept changing his mind about where he wanted his burial chamber to be. Others claim that these narrow passages and unusual caverns were carefully planned, perhaps for spiritual reasons or to prevent grave robbers. If anything is certain, it is that we may never truly know for sure!

On walls inside the inner chambers, (which were never meant to be seen), there are still some markings left by the original builders!

The King's Chamber is where Khufu himself would have been buried. Inside is a large stone sarcophagus, though its contents are long gone.

The Queen's Chamber probably never held a queen. It is more likely that this room held some of Khufu's belongings, which he may have been meant to carry into the afterlife.

When it was first built, the outside of the Great Pyramid was finished with smooth limestone, but sadly, most of this outer layer has since been stolen.

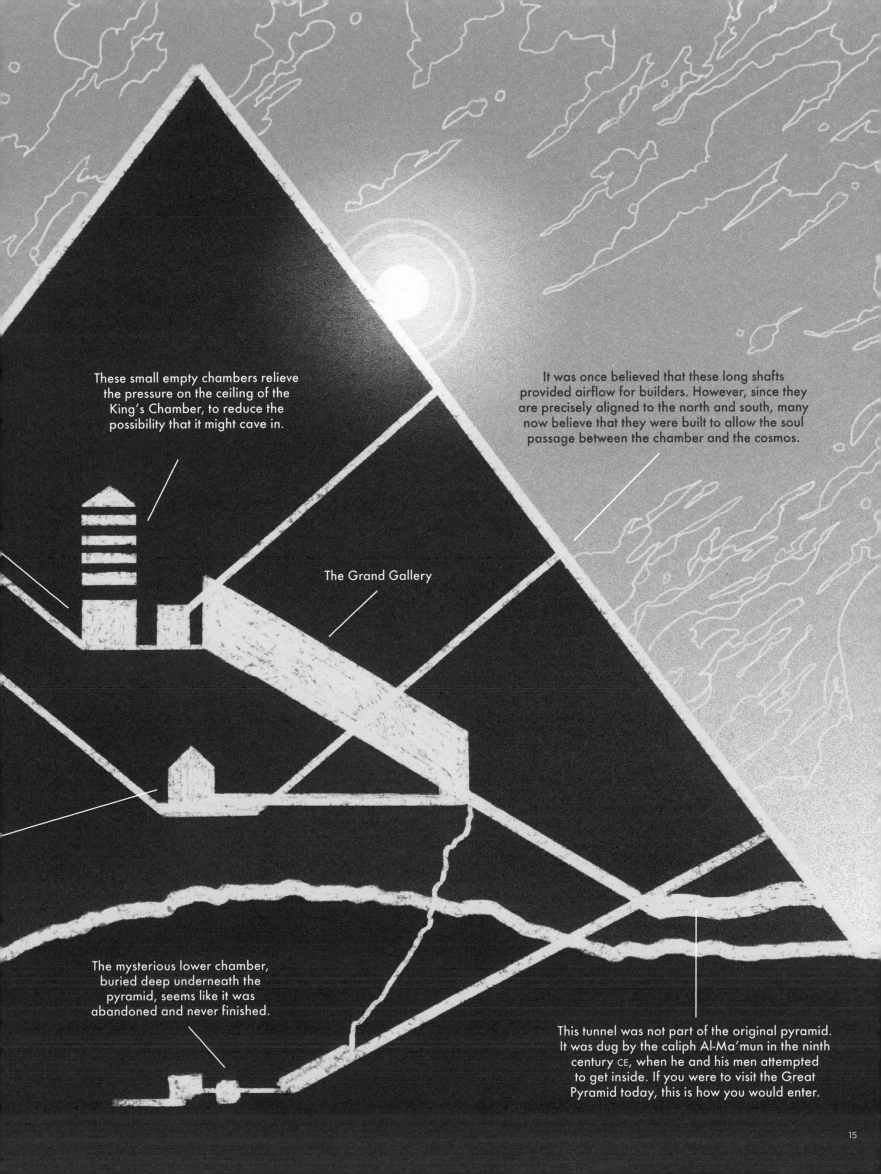

These small empty chambers relieve the pressure on the ceiling of the King's Chamber, to reduce the possibility that it might cave in.

It was once believed that these long shafts provided airflow for builders. However, since they are precisely aligned to the north and south, many now believe that they were built to allow the soul passage between the chamber and the cosmos.

The Grand Gallery

The mysterious lower chamber, buried deep underneath the pyramid, seems like it was abandoned and never finished.

This tunnel was not part of the original pyramid. It was dug by the caliph Al-Ma'mun in the ninth century CE, when he and his men attempted to get inside. If you were to visit the Great Pyramid today, this is how you would enter.

ANCIENT TECH: MOVING AND LIFTING

The builders of great ancient structures did not have modern machinery to lift and carry massive slabs of stone. It was ingenious maneuvering, and a few clever tricks of physics, that allowed them to make the most of the simple materials they had.

MOVING

To carry slabs of stone to the building site of the Great Pyramid, huge groups of builders dragged sleds across the ground. Each sledge might weigh several tons! As they went, workers would pour water ahead of the crew to form a smooth, firm path for the sled to slide on as it was dragged. This prevented the stone and sled from getting stuck in the desert sand.

Medieval builders in China used a similar system to carry massive stones nearly 45 miles to Beijing to build its Forbidden City. They worked through the dead of winter, wetting the surface of long paths of ice to help their sleds slip along.

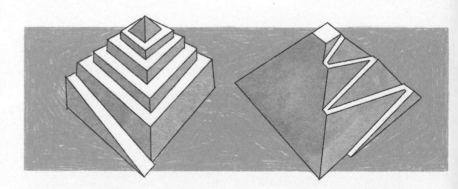

Many scholars agree that the builders of the Great Pyramid lifted stones by constructing ramps and dragging the stones up the sides of the pyramid on sleds. They would have then removed the ramps after the pyramid was completed.

LIFTING

The ancient Egyptians and Indians were some of the first to use levers. This simple but clever device allowed a single person to lift many times their own weight just by pressing down on the lever's long end.

The first recorded use of pulleys is in Mesopotamia, around 1500 BCE for lifting buckets of water. But it was the ancient Greeks, about 1,000 years later, who took this system and built the first crane, which allowed them to lift very heavy objects high up. The cranes took up a lot less space and required fewer laborers than a ramp.

ANOTHER WONDER: STONEHENGE

Circa 3000–2500 BCE

Although not considered an ancient wonder, Stonehenge is one of the world's most famous monuments, erected on Salisbury Plain in southern England centuries before the Great Pyramid at Giza was built. However, much about its purpose, and the people who built it, is shrouded in mystery.

Neolithic people began building Stonehenge around 3000 BCE, but it wasn't until several hundred years later that its stones were placed. The larger stones, called sarsen stones, weigh up to 66,000 pounds, and were probably cut from an area 20 miles away. Incredibly, the smaller stones, called bluestones, were transported from a spot nearly 155 miles away!

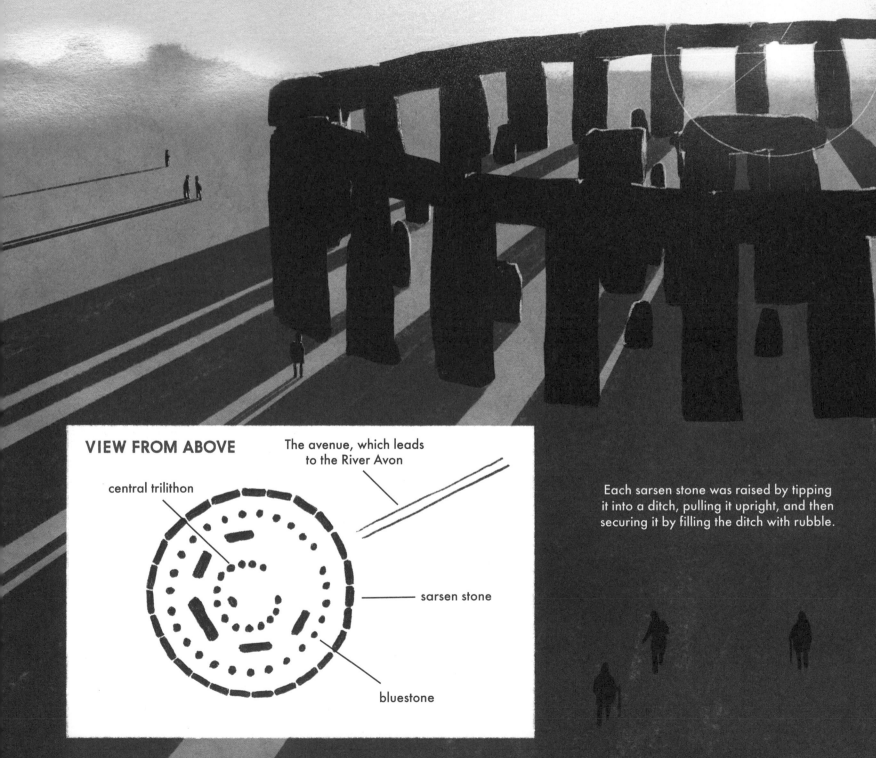

VIEW FROM ABOVE

The avenue, which leads to the River Avon

central trilithon

sarsen stone

bluestone

Each sarsen stone was raised by tipping it into a ditch, pulling it upright, and then securing it by filling the ditch with rubble.

Stonehenge is the site of many prehistoric burials and cremations. It may have been a place to lay the dead to rest, as well as a place to remember loved ones, much like a cemetery today.

The masterpiece was designed so that every year during the summer solstice, the sun rose exactly along the avenue, while during the winter solstice, the sun set directly between the two stones of the central trilithon.

The bluestone were probably raised into place by building stacked wooden platforms similar to scaffolding we use today.

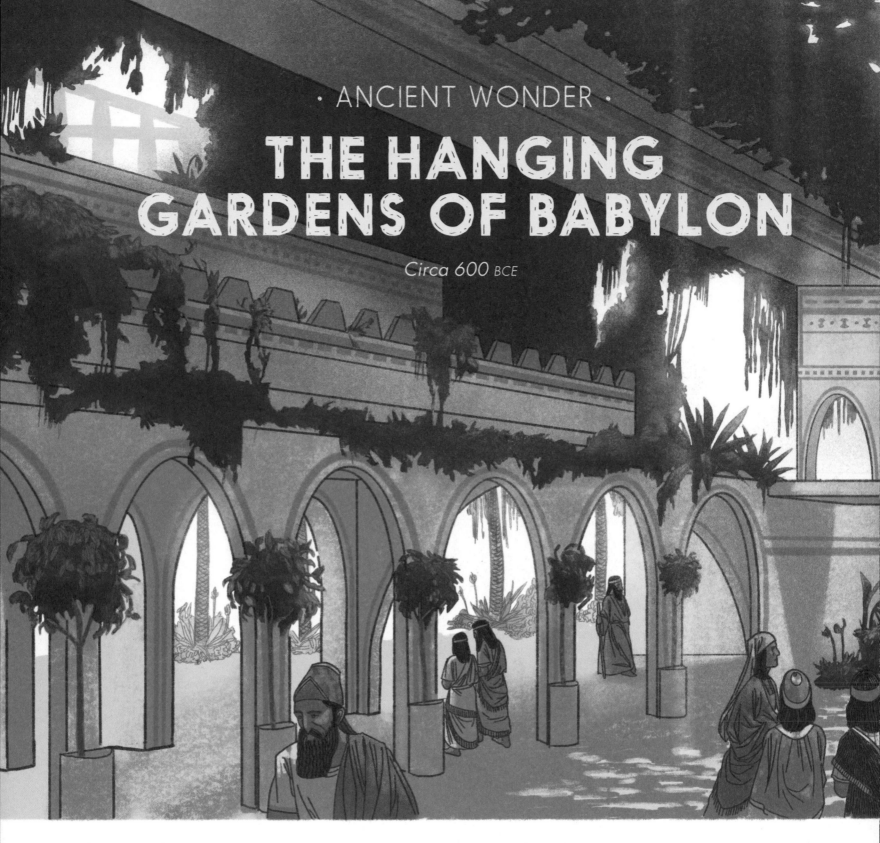

THE HANGING GARDENS OF BABYLON

Circa 600 BCE

Ancient travelers and historians tell of a vast hanging garden, blooming with lush greenery and streams of cool clear water, nestled in a world-renowned city. These are the Hanging Gardens of Babylon.

Word of these gardens traveled far and wide in the ancient world. It was said to have been a great intricate structure, with mighty trees suspended above stone archways. People marveled at its crisscrossing aqueducts and streams, seemingly flowing upward against gravity to nourish impossibly airborne gardens. Its construction was believed to be a gesture of love from the great Babylonian king Nebuchadnezzar II to his wife, Queen Amytis, who missed the greenery of her homeland.

These breathtaking gardens would have been an oasis to the people of the city of Babylon. But there is one catch to this alluring myth—it may have never existed at all.

Unlike other ancient wonders, no one has ever found a trace of the famous Hanging Gardens of Babylon. In fact, while Nebuchadnezzar wrote extensively about the grand palaces and gates that were built during his reign, he never mentions a word about any gardens. And while we have many elaborate descriptions of this wonder, they were all written by historians and writers who had never actually laid eyes on the gardens themselves. To this very day, we cannot know for sure if this ancient wonder once stood . . . or if it is simply the stuff of legend.

INSPIRATION: GARDENS OF PARADISE

The idea of a perfect, tranquil garden of paradise is quite familiar. People who practice Christianity, Judaism, or Islam may know the story of the beautiful Garden of Eden, where it is said that the first humans, called Adam and Eve, lived in harmony with all living things. In fact, these religions have their roots in the very same part of the world where the Hanging Gardens of Babylon are said to have been.

The Babylonians and their neighboring civilizations first settled in a region we now call the Fertile Crescent in Western Asia. The weather there was punishingly hot, but the great rivers Tigris and Euphrates often flooded and made perfect soil for farming. Some of the greatest cities in history were built here, and for their citizens, a bountiful garden and plentiful water meant food and life could flourish. It is no surprise that the ancient people of the Fertile Crescent spent many hot, dry days dreaming of lounging in a shady paradise.

23

ANCIENT TECH: WATERWAYS

Access to running water was one of the most important requirements for a great city. Without it, its people would have nothing to drink, could not irrigate their crops to grow food, and would have no way to get their waste away from the city. The great minds of the ancient world devised some truly ingenious ways to transport water over vast distances, across valleys, and up hills to reach their fellow citizens.

ARCHIMEDES' SCREW

This clever device is named after Archimedes, a famous ancient Greek scientist and mathematician. It uses a giant rotating screw inside of a pipe to pull water upward, helping to transport water uphill or into the upper stories of buildings. This is the device said to have been one of the secrets to the construction of the Hanging Gardens of Babylon.

SEWERS

In many ancient sewage systems, toilets would have direct access to a stream of running water, which would carry waste through the sewers and away from the city. The city of Lothal in India has one of the oldest sewage systems in the world, dating back 6,000 years.

The great sewer of Rome, called Cloaca Maxima, was so important to the ancient Romans that it even had its own goddess, called Cloacina.

AQUEDUCTS

Aqueducts carried water to a city from a faraway source—sometimes more than 60 miles away. Often these were below ground, but sometimes parts of them would be supported by enormous arched bridges to carry the water across valleys. The ancient Romans built some of the most famous aqueducts. They were so well built that they still stand today, nearly 2,000 years later!

ANOTHER WONDER: THE BANAUE RICE TERRACES

Circa 650 BCE–100 CE

A unique and inventive ancient form of irrigation can be found in the breathtaking Banaue Rice Terraces. These narrow, winding staircases of rice paddies were carved and molded into the mountainsides by the Ifugao people of the Philippines using very simple tools. They are said to have been built nearly 2,000 years ago, and have been in continuous use ever since to grow rice and vegetables.

Normally, rice is farmed in large, flat areas with lots of water. But the land occupied by the Ifugao people was mostly very steep . . . so they had to get creative. The Ifugao people carved an ingenious system of terraces into the mountainside, which allowed them to use every inch of land for farming. When heavy rains fell on the forested mountaintops, the complex web of carved channels and bamboo pipes carried the water downhill and distributed it to the paddies, which need to stay flooded in order for rice to grow properly.

There are just over 3,800 square miles of rice paddies at Banaue. If these narrow terraces were all lined up end to end, they would cover half of the circumference of the entire Earth!

· ANCIENT WONDER ·

THE TEMPLE OF ARTEMIS AT EPHESUS

Circa 550 BCE

Artemis was considered the bravest and wisest huntress, a shining symbol of strength and womanhood. For those who followed and worshipped this goddess, Ephesus was home to the ultimate tribute to her glory.

The Temple of Artemis was one of the first structures ever to be built entirely of marble, and was nearly three times the size of the Parthenon in Athens, Greece. It was clad in the most stunning artwork that many worshippers had ever seen—beautiful carvings adorned the bases of many of its 120 grand columns and superb friezes ran across its top. Inside, statues of mythical warrior women known as Amazonians were displayed as well as an altar to the goddess Artemis and a statue of her for worshippers to admire.

This great marvel met its tragic demise in the middle of the fourth century BCE, when a local man called Herostratus burned it to the ground in an attempt to gain eternal infamy. Indeed, he was forever known as the arsonist who destroyed this iconic place of worship. Happily, the temple was soon rebuilt, and this version survived until the third century CE, when it was finally destroyed by invaders.

Today, nearly all that remains of this great monument lies in a small field to the west of Selçuk in Turkey . . . a few piles of rubble and a feeble pillar, mere echoes of what they once were.

INSPIRATION: ARTEMIS, GODDESS OF THE HUNT

Artemis was a beloved goddess. She was the daughter of the god Zeus, and the twin sister of Apollo, god of the arts and knowledge. Sprinting swiftly through forests with a deer at her side and a bow and arrow at her back, she was the greatest of all hunters and archers, as well as the brave guardian of animals and nature. She was also a strong symbol of womanhood, protecting young girls and guiding women through childbirth.

Artemis was revered so widely and so passionately that she came to be known by many names throughout the ancient world. Greeks sometimes knew her as Phoebe or Cynthia, and the Romans knew her as Diana. The Ephesians had their own particular version of Artemis, which looked a bit different from her traditional Greek image.

This Ephesian Artemis probably resembles the statue at the shrine of the Temple of Artemis, though nothing of it survives today.

ANOTHER WONDER: THE ELLORA CAVES

Circa 600–1000 CE

Not all temples are built from the ground up. Some, like the Ellora Caves in western India, are carved into the very cliffs themselves. This exquisitely detailed, winding complex of more than 34 temples and monasteries was carved over hundreds of years by gifted artists who wished to honor their kings and gods. It is a hauntingly beautiful place, where pilgrims of the Buddhist, Hindu, and Jain religions all have spaces to worship in harmony.

Kailasanatha, or Kailasa, is a Hindu temple, and one of the largest at the Ellora Caves.

KAILASA TEMPLE

This magnificent excavated temple is dedicated to the Hindu god Shiva, and was carved from a single, enormous rock. The central shrine to Shiva was probably inspired by Mount Kailash, a huge mountain in the Himalayas that has great importance to worshippers of many different religions.

ALL-SEEING DEITY

Hindu legend tells that the omnipresent god, Shiva, sits alongside his wife Parvati at the top of Mount Kailash, where he keeps watch over the world for all eternity.

Ravana is shown lifting Mount Kailash from beneath.

KING OF THE DEMONS

Ravana is the many-headed god, who in Hinduism is known as king of the demons. Legend tells that Ravana, eager to show his strength, once tried to lift Mount Kailash, but Shiva trapped him beneath it, where he stayed for a thousand years.

Nandi is also the guardian spirit of Mount Kailash.

GUARDIAN SPIRIT

Belonging to Shiva, Nandi is a sacred bull who symbolizes strength and bears truth. He is often seen guarding shrines to his beloved god.

THE STATUE OF ZEUS AT OLYMPIA

Circa 430 BCE

Towering over onlookers, the magnificent statue of Zeus at Olympia stood for more than 800 years, inspiring awe and amazement in those who came to worship before it.

This great statue was a larger-than-life chryselephantine sculpture, meaning it used finely chiseled ivory for skin and hammered gold for hair and robes. In one hand the great Zeus held a small statue of Nike, the goddess of victory, and in the other he held a tall, jewel-encrusted scepter topped with a golden eagle. The statue's throne stood above a great black stone pool filled with olive oil, which would reflect the light of the sun coming from outside and cast a golden glow throughout the hallowed space. The olive oil would have collected in the pool after being poured over the statue. This was done regularly to prevent the ivory from drying out and cracking.

The monument was sculpted by Phidias, the most famous sculptor of his age. It seems that his work was so widely appreciated that his workshop, which stood nearby, was preserved in honor of his creative genius.

The fate of the great statue of Zeus is a mystery: some historians believe that it was moved to the ancient city of Constantinople, where it was destroyed in a great fire soon after. Others believe that it was destroyed along with its temple when Christian emperors of Rome tried to eliminate monuments to pagan gods. Whatever the truth, all that we have left of this great wonder are the starry-eyed accounts of the lucky people who lived to see it.

INSPIRATION: ZEUS, KING OF THE GODS

The mighty Zeus, chief of the Greek pantheon, ruled over gods and humans alike from his perch atop the majestic Mount Olympus. The threat of his wicked temper and powerful lightning bolts was enough to strike fear into the heart of anyone so unwise as to defy him. Zeus was so widely revered that the Romans continued to worship him after the Greeks, although they knew him by the name Jupiter instead.

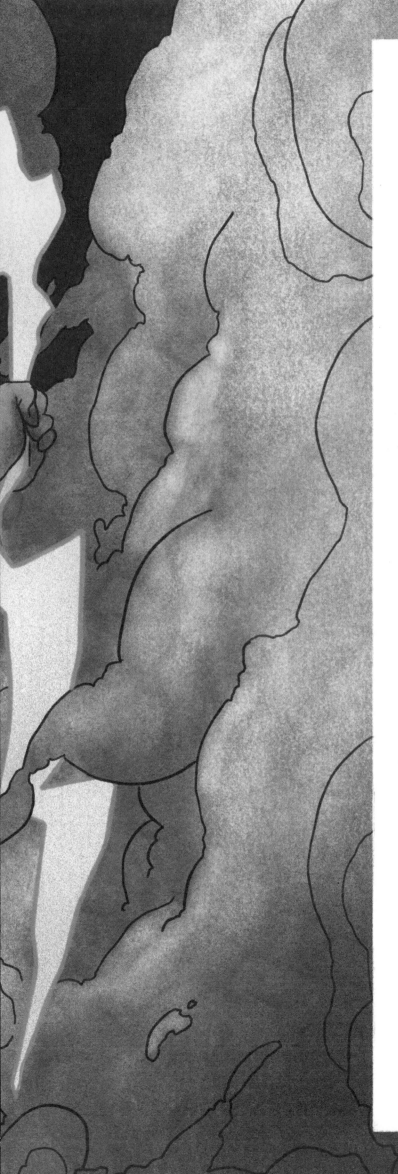

According to legend, Zeus is the son of the titan Cronus, and the grandson of Gaia and Uranus, the gods of the earth and sky. Cronus, who feared that Zeus and his other children would turn against him, ate each of his children as soon as they were born. But Zeus, the youngest, managed to escape, and when he grew strong enough, defeated his father and rescued all of his siblings from Cronus's greedy belly.

Zeus went on to rule with his two brothers. While he ruled the skies, his brother Poseidon ruled the seas and his brother Hades ruled the underworld. Zeus fathered many of the famous gods and heroes of Greek mythology.

ANCIENT TECH: BUILDING BIG

History's biggest sculptures are often the most impressive . . . and were also probably the most difficult to build. With materials that were heavy or expensive, often the true genius of these feats of engineering is invisible to the naked eye.

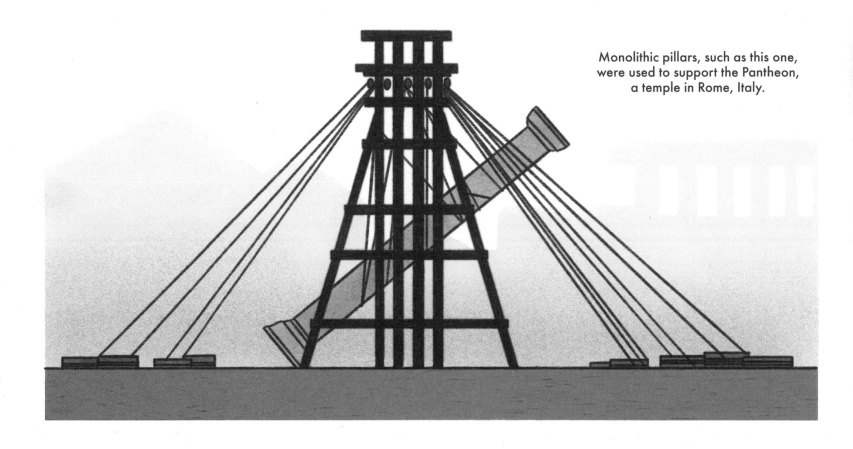

Monolithic pillars, such as this one, were used to support the Pantheon, a temple in Rome, Italy.

THE COLUMN PROBLEM

In ancient times, building the strong stone columns that still stand today was no small task. Some builders, like the ancient Romans, preferred monolithic pillars. This meant that the entire pillar was sculpted out of a single piece of stone, and then, incredibly, lifted into place by a crane called a "trispastos" or a "polyspastos."

In ancient Greece, it was more common to build columns in sections called "drums." These smaller pieces of stone were easier to transport, and could be lifted and stacked on top of each other by cranes.

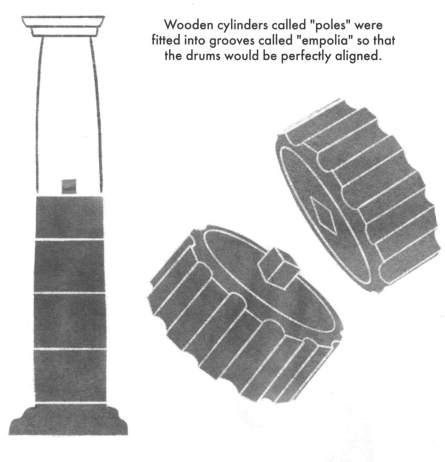

Wooden cylinders called "poles" were fitted into grooves called "empolia" so that the drums would be perfectly aligned.

ZEUS AT OLYMPIA

Although the great statue of Zeus was created with expensive, precious materials, Phidias had to make use of something much more common to construct the interior—wood.

This massive statue was actually hollow, with a wooden skeleton that made it quite sturdy, light, and cheap to build. The delicate gold and ivory were then laid on top in thin layers and sculpted by hand. By the time Phidias had finished, it would have seemed as though the glistening Zeus had been carved from unimaginably large blocks of ivory and gold.

THE MAUSOLEUM AT HALICARNASSUS

Circa 353–350 BCE

The word "mausoleum" refers to a grand monument that marks the tomb of an important person. The very idea of a mausoleum came from a single person—King Mausolus of Caria (now known as modern-day Turkey).

From the moment he became ruler of Caria in 377 BCE, Mausolus began constructing a stunning new capital city at Halicarnassus. At the center of all of this new work was a plan for a grand monument, the likes of which no one in the ancient world had yet seen—Mausolus's own tomb. With some of the most accomplished builders and artisans at that time, construction began on the great mausoleum—until the king died just a few years later.

Mausolus was buried in his half-finished tomb, but the construction didn't stop there. His grief-stricken wife, Artemisia II, devoted herself to enshrining her late husband, and commissioned the most stunning tomb the world had ever seen. Even Artemisia did not live to see the tomb completed, but its dedicated artisans continued even after her death. The result was a mausoleum so breathtaking that word of it traveled far and wide. Massive friezes stretched across the faces of the tomb, depicting the glory of famous battles and legends. It stood proudly above Halicarnassus for nearly 1,700 years until, historians believe, a series of earthquakes brought it crashing to the ground.

INSPIRATION: HONORING THE DEAD

Across almost every part of the globe, skilled ancient builders and craftspeople devoted enormous amounts of time and effort to building beautiful structures in memory of their departed loved ones and rulers. It is a passion that seems to be shared by humans no matter where they come from, and the results of these efforts, even thousands of years ago, can still be seen today.

ANGKOR WAT, ANGKOR, CAMBODIA, CIRCA 1113–1145 CE

This temple is one of the largest religious monuments in the world, and was originally built to honor the Hindu god Vishnu.

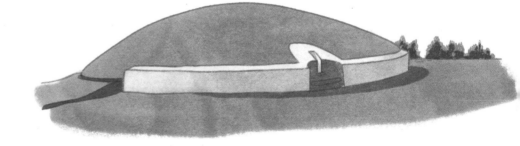

MEGALITHIC TOMB OF NEWGRANGE, COUNTY MEATH, IRELAND, CIRCA 3200 BCE

Older than the Great Pyramid of Giza, and even Stone Henge, this enormous mound was thought to have been constructed during the Stone Age.

SAMANID MAUSOLEUM, BUKHARA, UZBEKISTAN, 892–943 CE

This stunning temple is the resting place of Ismail Samani, the founder of the Samanid dynasty.

TEMPLE OF THE INSCRIPTIONS, PALENQUE, MEXICO, CIRCA 675–702 CE

Set in the Mexican jungle, this beautiful temple features carved hieroglyphs and pictures by the ancient Maya.

ROYAL TOMBS, PETRA, JORDAN, CIRCA 200 BCE–100 CE

The Nabataean carved these tombs from sandstone, possibly for the kings and queens of the ancient city.

CASTEL SANT'ANGELO, ROME, ITALY, 135–139 CE

Also known as the Mausoleum of Hadrian, this tomb was originally commissioned by the Roman emperor Hadrian, and his ashes were interred here after his death.

Circa 210 BCE

Few mausoleums are as enormous or well-guarded as the burial site of Qin Shi Huang, the first emperor of China. In fact, a devoted army of over 8,000 soldiers has been guarding the final resting place of their ruler since his death more than 2,000 years ago. Diligent in their watch, they have stood without flinching, without sleeping, without eating or drawing a breath . . . though this is not surprising, because they are all made of clay.

PAINTED WARRIORS

This famous Terracotta Army is an incredible feat of craftsmanship. Foot soldiers, generals, chariots, and horses all stand in formation, cheered on by performers and military officials.

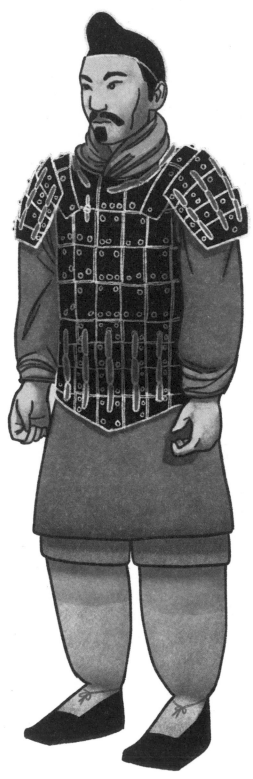

Today, most of these figures are the same color as the earth around them, but at the time of their creation, these ranks of loyal subjects would have been painted with brilliant glazes in a spectacular, seemingly endless, sea of color.

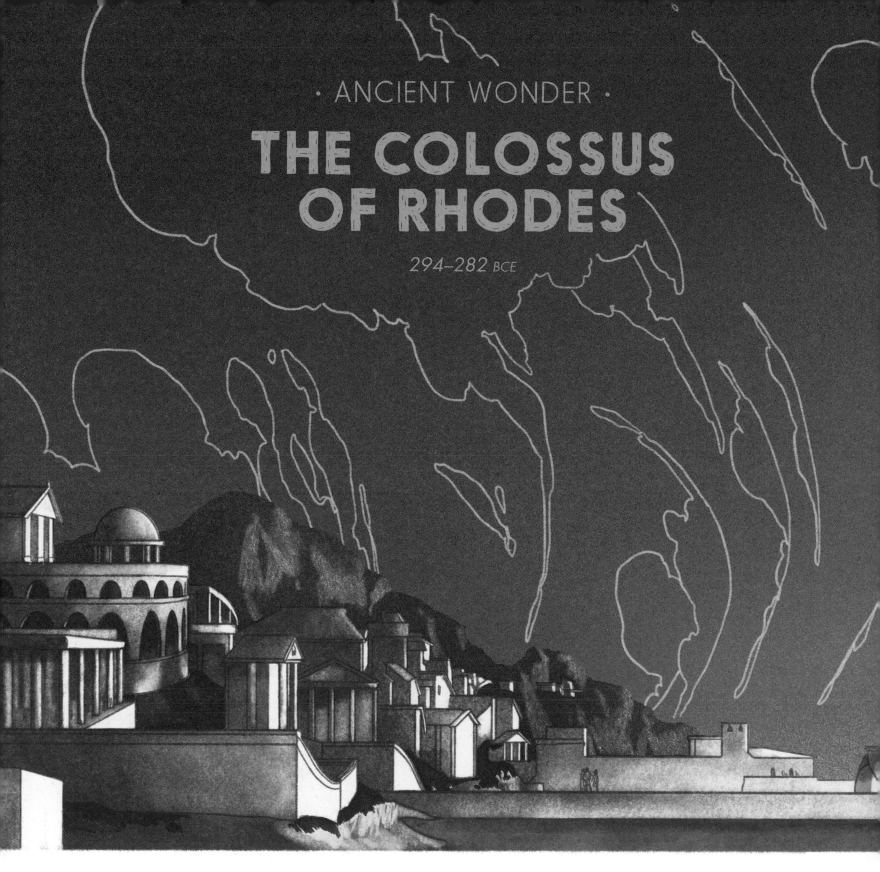

THE COLOSSUS OF RHODES

294–282 BCE

In 305 BCE, the very relieved people of the city of Rhodes had just thwarted a siege of their city at the hands of Demetrius of Syria. Grateful and proud, they decided to build a monument to thank Helios, god of the sun, who they believed was the guardian of their city. And so began the construction of the Colossus of Rhodes.

No one knows precisely what the Colossus looked like. We have no written descriptions of it and no artwork from the time that shows what position it stood in. Some historical illustrations show the Colossus standing with one leg on either side of the harbor, straddling the entrance as boats travel beneath it. While it makes a stunning image, today we know that it would have been physically impossible. It is likely to have stood to one side of the harbor.

We do know, though, that it was a truly enormous bronze statue of Helios, welcoming visitors and homecomers to Rhodes. At around 100 feet tall, it took nearly 12 years of careful building to be completed.

The magnificent Colossus left a lasting impression on all who saw it, but sadly it only stood for a mere fifty years before a terrible earthquake destroyed it.

INSPIRATION: HELIOS, GOD OF THE SUN

Tearing across the sky in his dazzling four-horse chariot, Helios the sun god burns brightly before diving beneath the horizon at day's end. In the Greek pantheon, he is worshipped as the embodiment of the sun, an all-seeing deity who watches from his home in the sky.

According to mythology, Helios was angry that the other gods had not given him any land to rule, and so Zeus promised him the island of Rhodes, which still lay under the sea. But just as he spoke, the island of Rhodes emerged from the sea lush and beautiful, and with it the nymph Rhodos, daughter of Poseidon. Helios fell in love instantly, drenching the island in his warm rays. He and Rhodos went on to have many children called the Heliadae, who became famous Rhodian seafarers and astrologers and founded many historic cities on the island of Rhodes.

ANCIENT TECH: BRONZE

Whether for sculptures as grand as the Colossus of Rhodes or as humble as a common water jug, the ability to make tools and artworks out of bronze was a crucial part of the development of ancient societies. Stronger and more durable than copper or stone, bronze could also be used to make better tools, weapons, and armor. It was so important, in fact, that it gave its name to the Bronze Age, a time from just before 3000 BCE up until around 500 BCE when many civilizations were producing a lot of bronze objects.

Bronze is a mixture of copper, tin, and small pieces of other metals. To mix the metals, they have to be heated so much that they become a liquid. They are then mixed together and poured into a mold, or allowed to cool and then hammered into shape.

LOST WAX BRONZE CASTING

Sculptures in bronze were created through a process called lost wax casting.

The artist would first create their artwork in wax, and then cover it in a thick outer clay coating.

When this was heated, the outer coating hardened and the wax melted, creating a perfect cast of the sculpture.

Finally, molten liquid bronze, which had been heated to about 2,200°F, was poured into the mold.

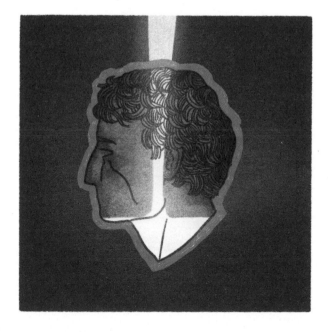

After it had cooled, the outer clay coating was broken, and within it was the final bronze sculpture.

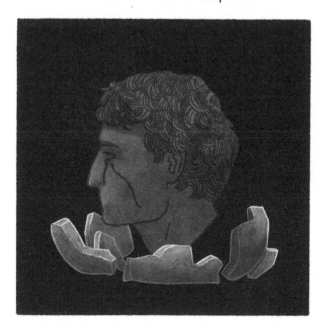

Larger bronze works would have been cast in smaller sections. These would then be transported to the final building site, and the sculpture would have been assembled piece by piece.

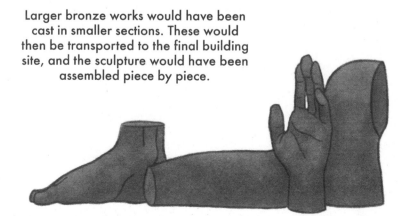

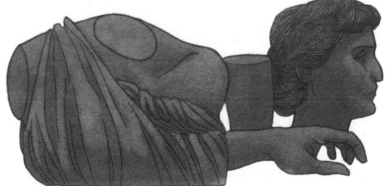

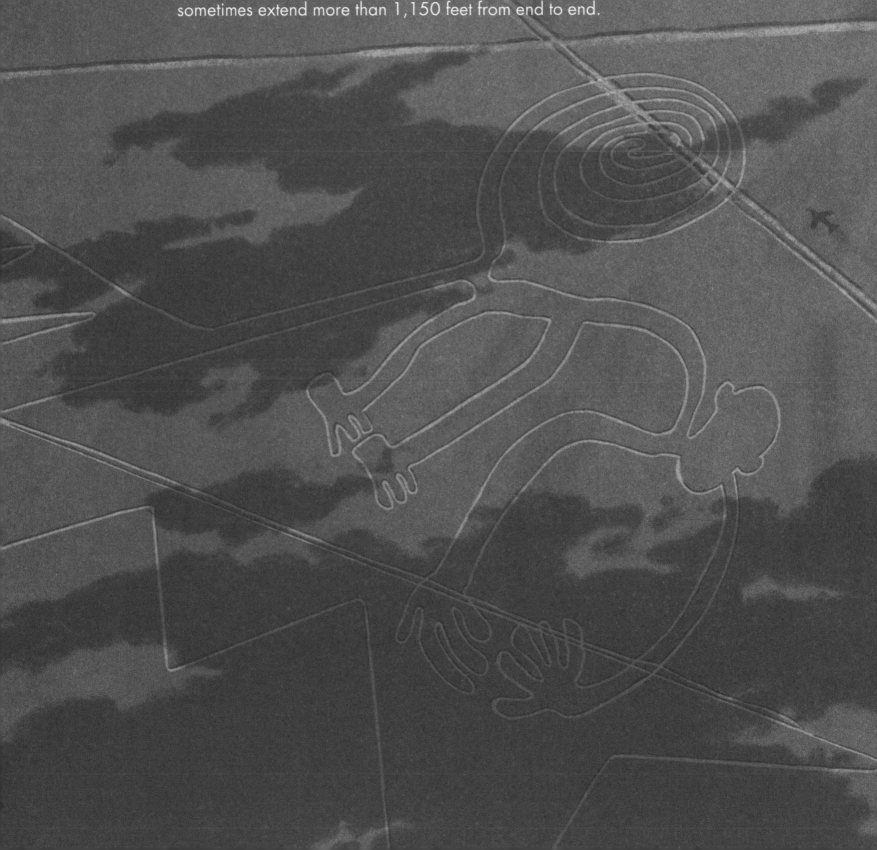

ANOTHER WONDER: THE NAZCA LINES

Circa 200 BCE–700 CE

Building big does not always mean building tall. Etched across vast stretches of the south Peruvian desert are a web of curious earthworks—lines carved into the sand-varnished surface, some nearly 2,000 years old. These are the quietly mysterious Nazca Lines.

To an observer on the ground, it would simply seem that these carved paths crisscrossed at random. But seen from the sky or even a tall hill, these markings come to life, forming enormous images of animals and geometric shapes that sometimes extend more than 1,150 feet from end to end.

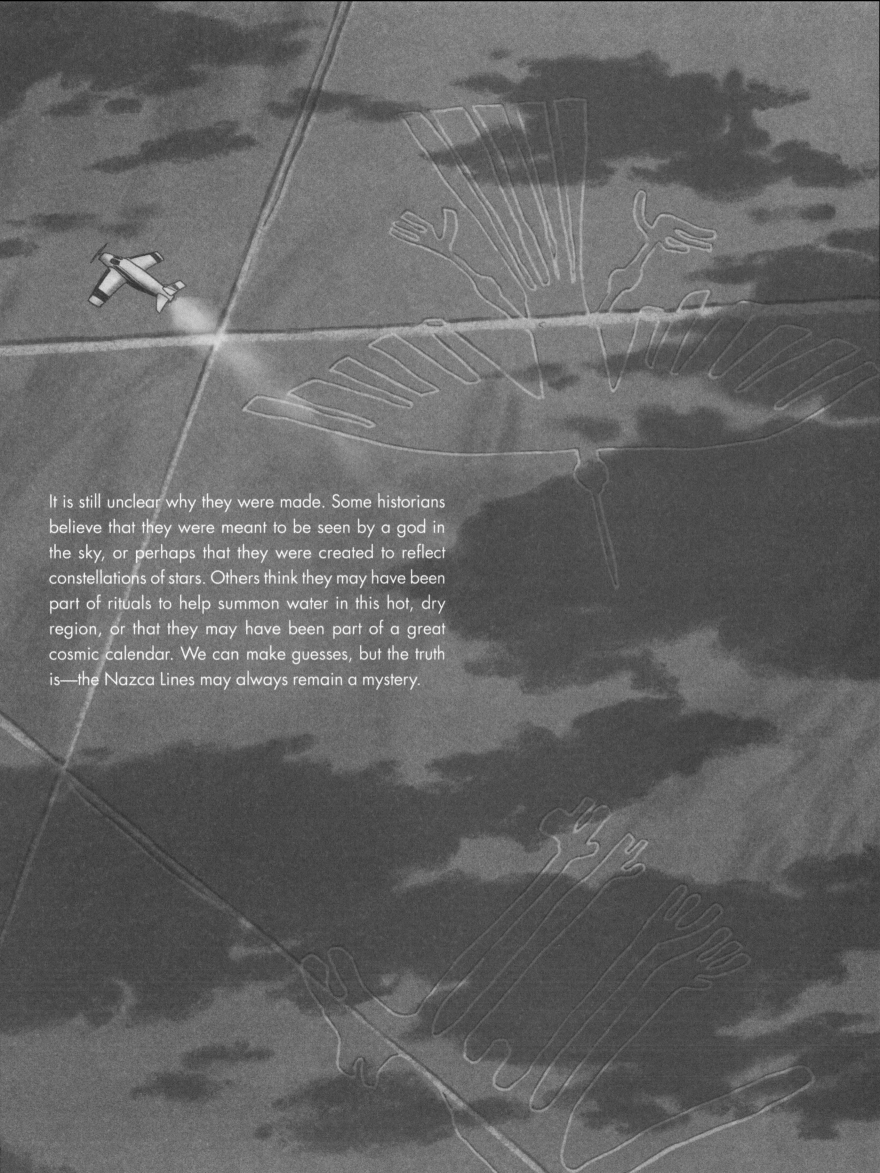

It is still unclear why they were made. Some historians believe that they were meant to be seen by a god in the sky, or perhaps that they were created to reflect constellations of stars. Others think they may have been part of rituals to help summon water in this hot, dry region, or that they may have been part of a great cosmic calendar. We can make guesses, but the truth is—the Nazca Lines may always remain a mystery.

THE LIGHTHOUSE OF ALEXANDRIA

Circa 300–280 BCE

From the third century BCE onward, a weary seafaring crew making their way in the dark to the legendary city of Alexandria, Egypt would have been greeted by a welcome sight—the beacon of the Lighthouse of Alexandria. Built during the reign of the rulers Ptolemy I and Ptolemy II, it was the second tallest structure in the ancient world after the Great Pyramid of Giza. It symbolized the thriving city, and contained its own small community of people.

At the base of the lighthouse were lodgings for soldiers, horses, and workers who cared for the lighthouse. Its shining white walls of granite and limestone concealed a spiral of stairs that led up to a second level, where citizens could enjoy stunning views of the ocean.

At the very top was the beacon itself. During the day, a mirror would reflect the light of the sun to direct ships approaching the harbor. The reflector probably had a curved surface, an important technological advance that would help direct an intense beam of light in a particular direction. At night, its light would come from an enormous bonfire. Dedicated caretakers would have to carry fuel up the high tower at all hours of the night to ensure that its guiding light would never go out.

The lighthouse guided weary travelers home from its perch in the Alexandrian harbor for over a thousand years, until earthquakes reduced it to just a stub.

Circa 331 BCE

Though only its lighthouse made it onto the famous list of seven ancient wonders, the city of Alexandria was a wonder in itself. It was founded around 331 BCE by the famously undefeated general, Alexander the Great, and soon became a haven for the greatest minds of the ancient world.

Greek mathematician Euclid, used transformation to prove that two triangles can be congruent.

MUSAEUM

Philosophers, mathematicians, scientists, poets, musicians, and many others flocked to the Musaeum at Alexandria. This research center was a melting pot of cultures and ideas, where huge numbers of thoughtful academic minds could live under one roof and study together. Where Euclid invented what we now know as geometry, Archimedes would, years later, spend his life developing early ideas about engineering.

The great scientist Archimedes, was able to discover the volume of a golden crown by measuring how much water it displaced when dropped in a tub.

Much of what we know about the ancient world, we owe to the dedicated Musaeum scholars. They spent their lives creating great works, as well as translating important poems, epic stories and songs from other languages to ensure that they would not be forgotten. All of this work was stored in the vast halls of the Library of Alexandria, which likely had hundreds of thousands of documents.

Tragically, the library suffered from at least two great fires. By 391 CE, nearly all of its carefully collected contents had been lost.

TIMELINE

This timeline shows the approximate longevity of each of the seven wonders, from completion to ruin. Incredibly, at the time of the Colossus of Rhodes all seven structures were still standing. Only the Great Pyramid of Giza still stands today.

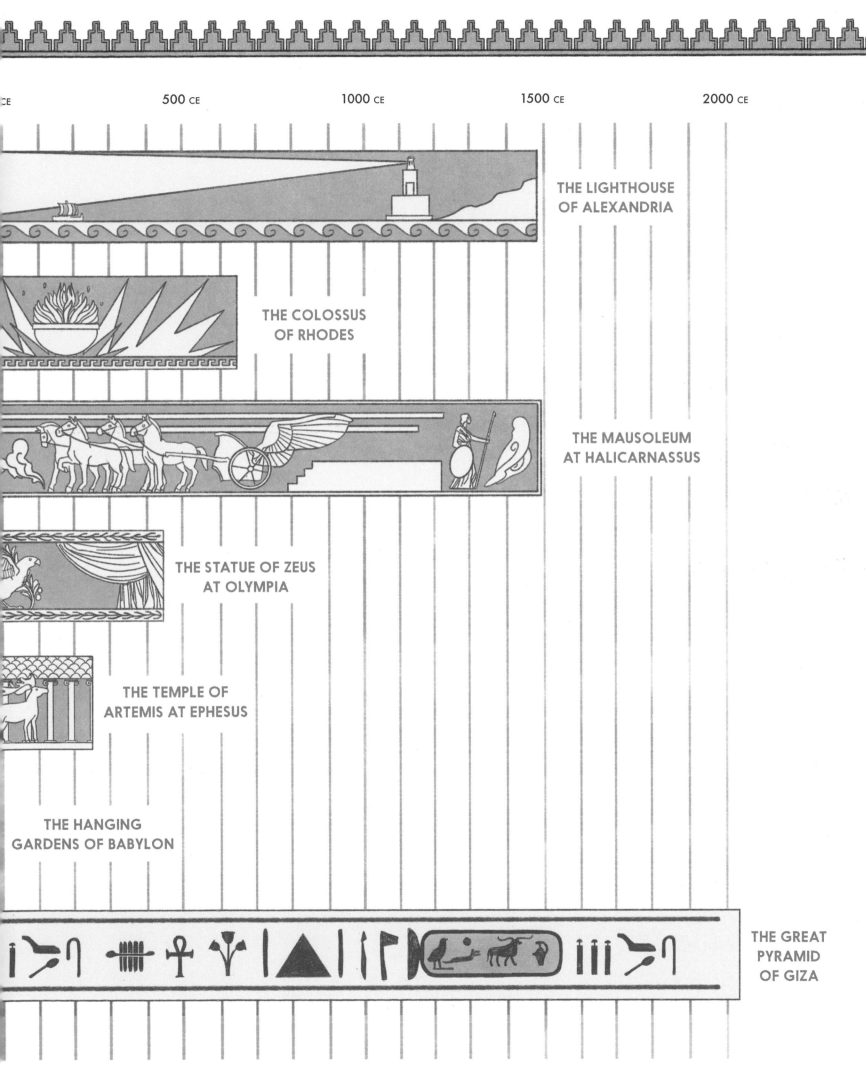

THE LIGHTHOUSE
OF ALEXANDRIA

THE COLOSSUS
OF RHODES

THE MAUSOLEUM
AT HALICARNASSUS

THE STATUE OF ZEUS
AT OLYMPIA

THE TEMPLE OF
ARTEMIS AT EPHESUS

THE HANGING
GARDENS OF BABYLON

THE GREAT
PYRAMID
OF GIZA

# INDEX